The Best of The Chieftains

ISBN 1-4234-1459-4

HAL•LEONARD®
CORPORATION
7777 W. BLUEMOUND RD. P.O. BOX 13819 MILWAUKEE, WI 53213

For all works contained herein:
Unauthorized copying, arranging, adapting, recording or public performance is an infringement of copyright.
Infringers are liable under the law.

Visit Hal Leonard Online at
www.halleonard.com

Music arranged by Roger Day.
Music processed by Paul Ewers Music Design.
Photos courtesy of LFI and Retna.
Printed in the United Kingdom

Up Against The Buachalawns

By M. Molloy.

Moderato - accel.

D.%. al Coda
To Coda ⊕

⊕ *Coda*

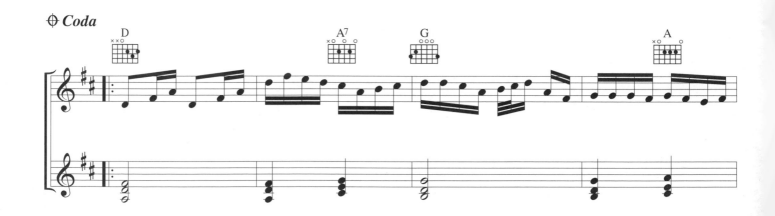

Boil The Breakfast Early

By P. Moloney.

Friel's Kitchen

Traditional. Arranged by S. Keane.

1.　　　　　　　　**2.**

D.%. al Coda
(with repeats)

To Coda ⊕

⊕ ***Coda***

♩. = **90**

accel.

1.　　　　　　　　**2.**

No.6 The Coombe

Traditional. Arranged by S. Potts.

Moderately - ad lib.

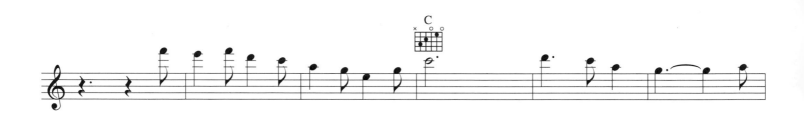

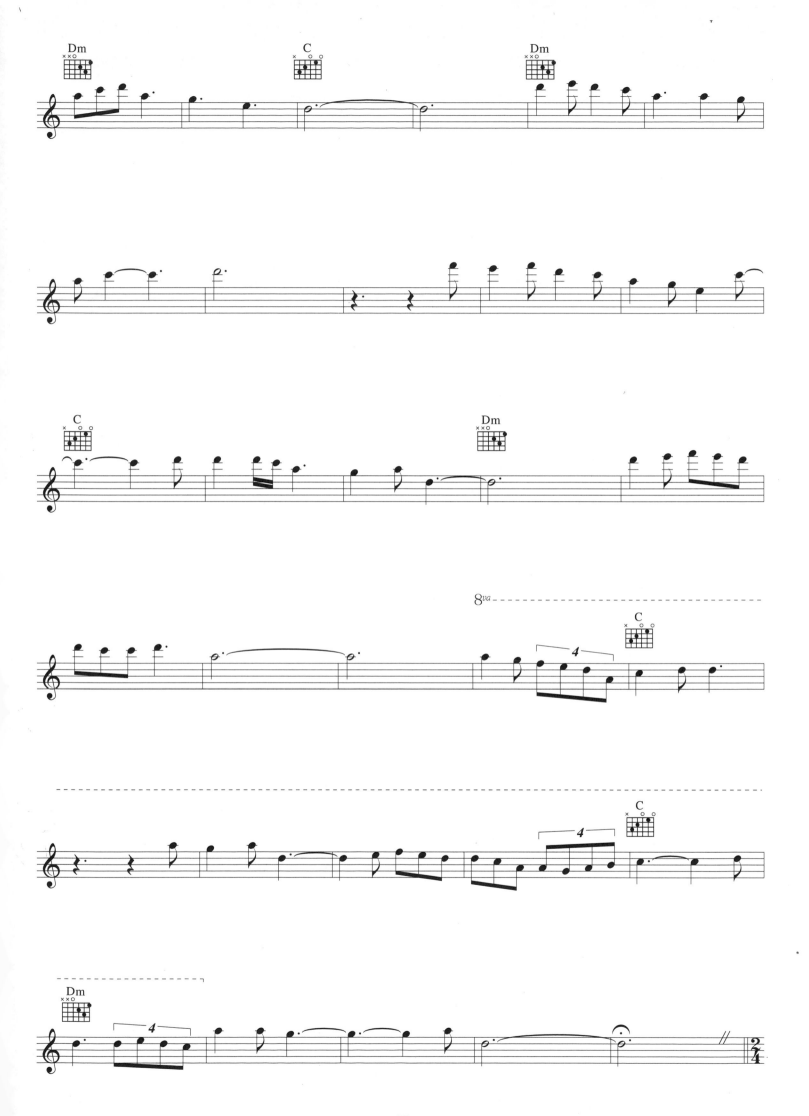

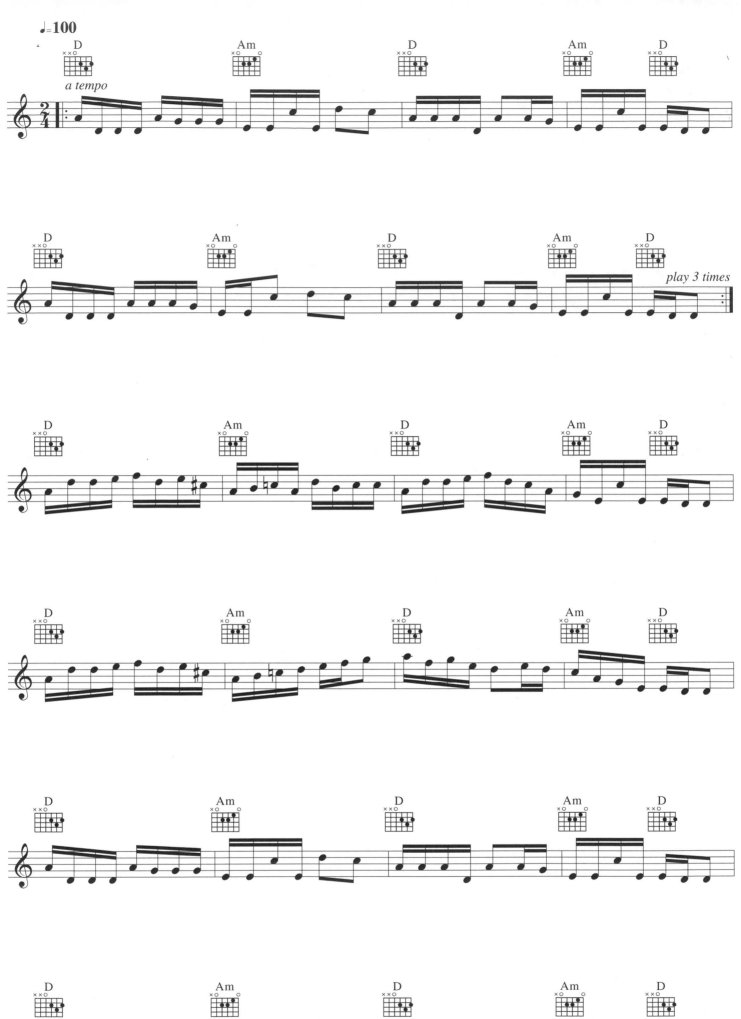

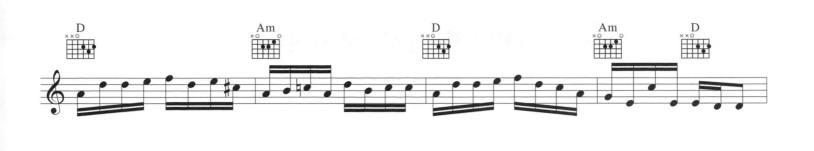

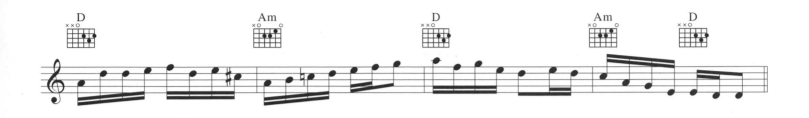

play 3 times

O'Sullivan's March

Traditional. Arranged by M. Tubridy.

Sea Image

By P. Moloney.

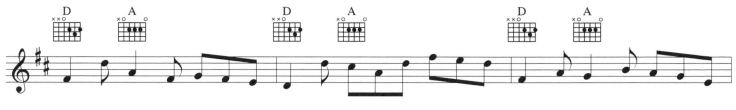

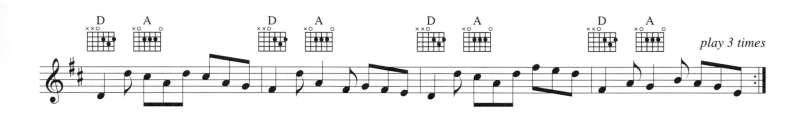

play 3 times

ad lib.

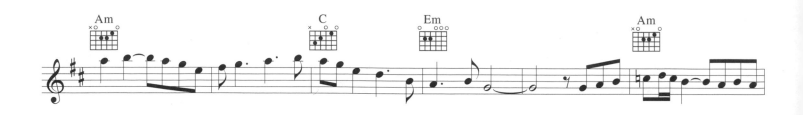

♩. = 102

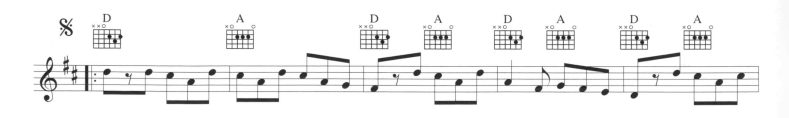

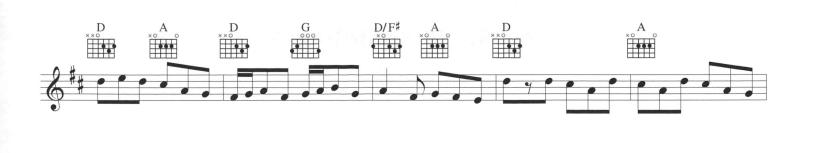

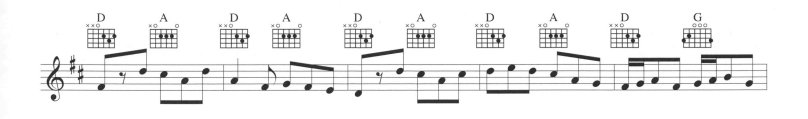

To Coda ⊕

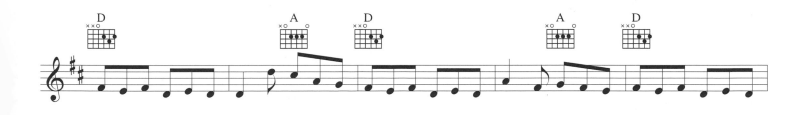

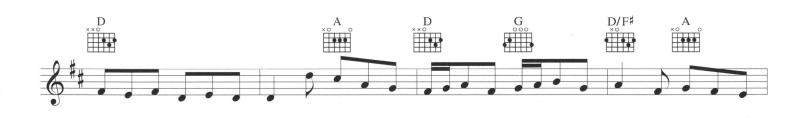

D.%. al Coda ⊕ *Coda*

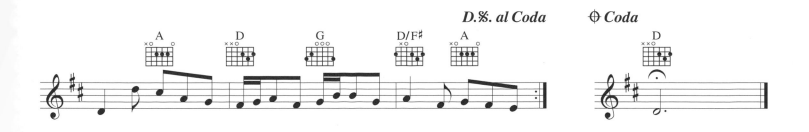

An Speic Seoigheach

By P. Moloney.

The Dogs Among The Bushes

Traditional. Arranged by S. Keane.

The Job Of Journeywork

Traditional. Arranged by M. Fay.

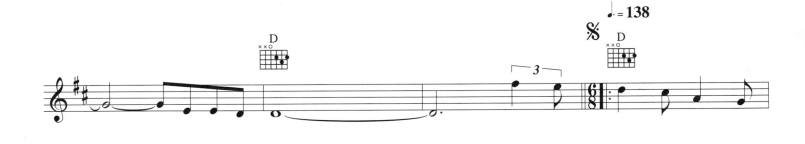

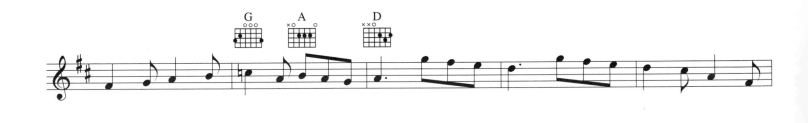

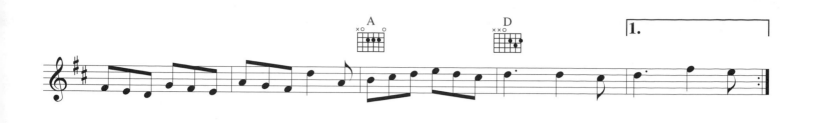

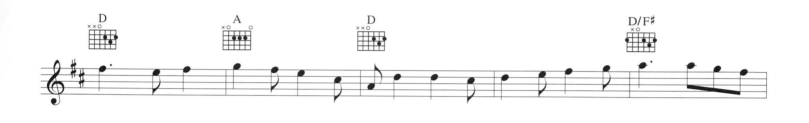

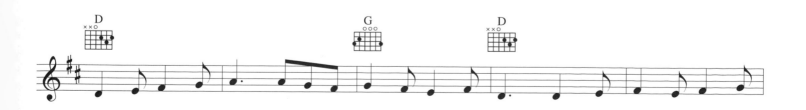

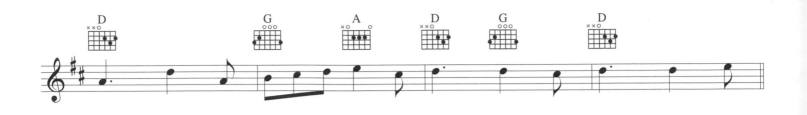

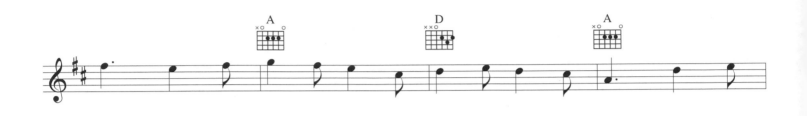

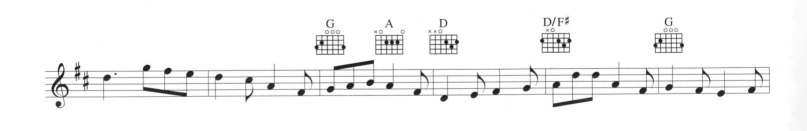

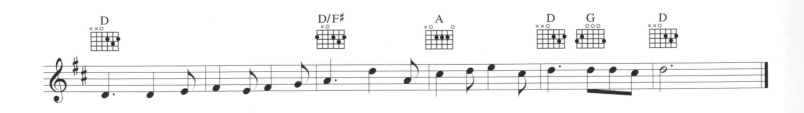

Oh! The Breeches Full Of Stitches

Traditional. Arranged by M. Tubridy.

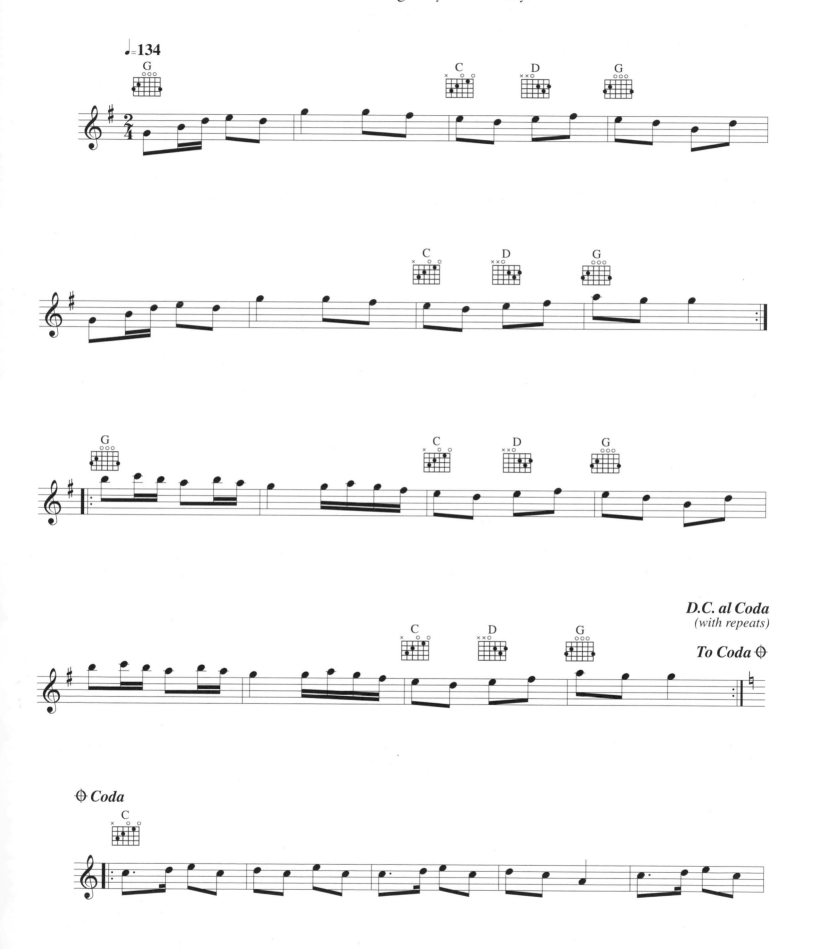

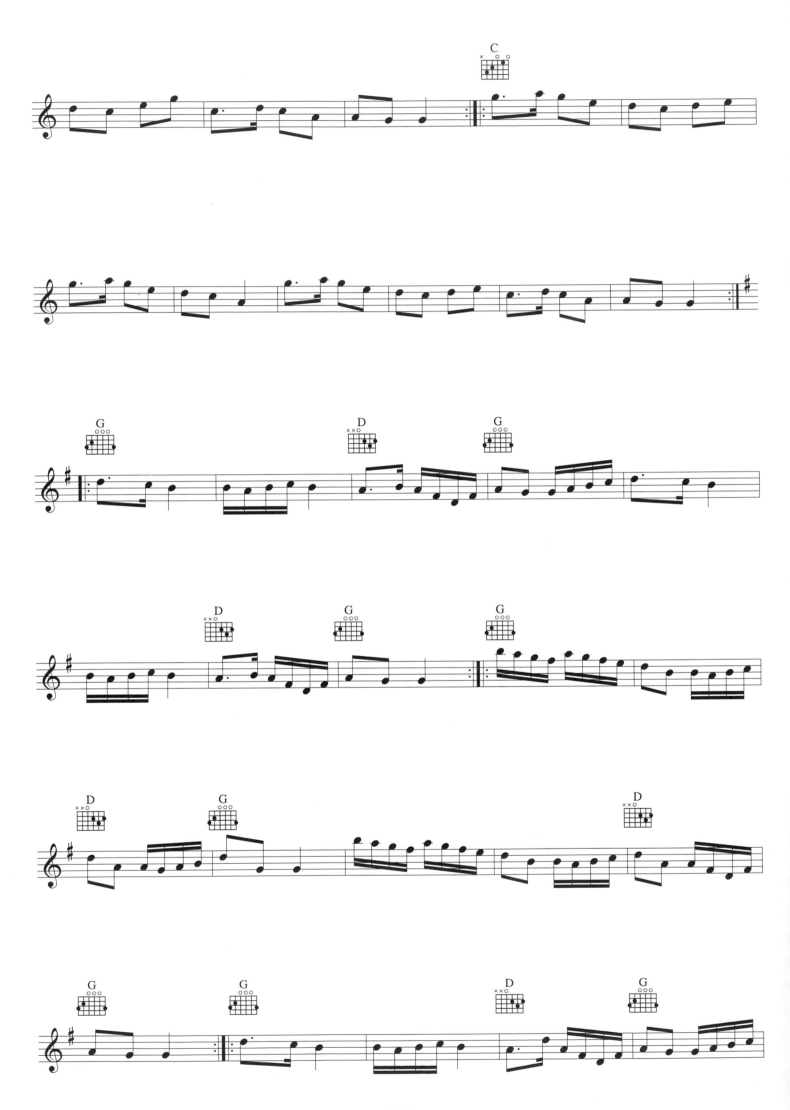

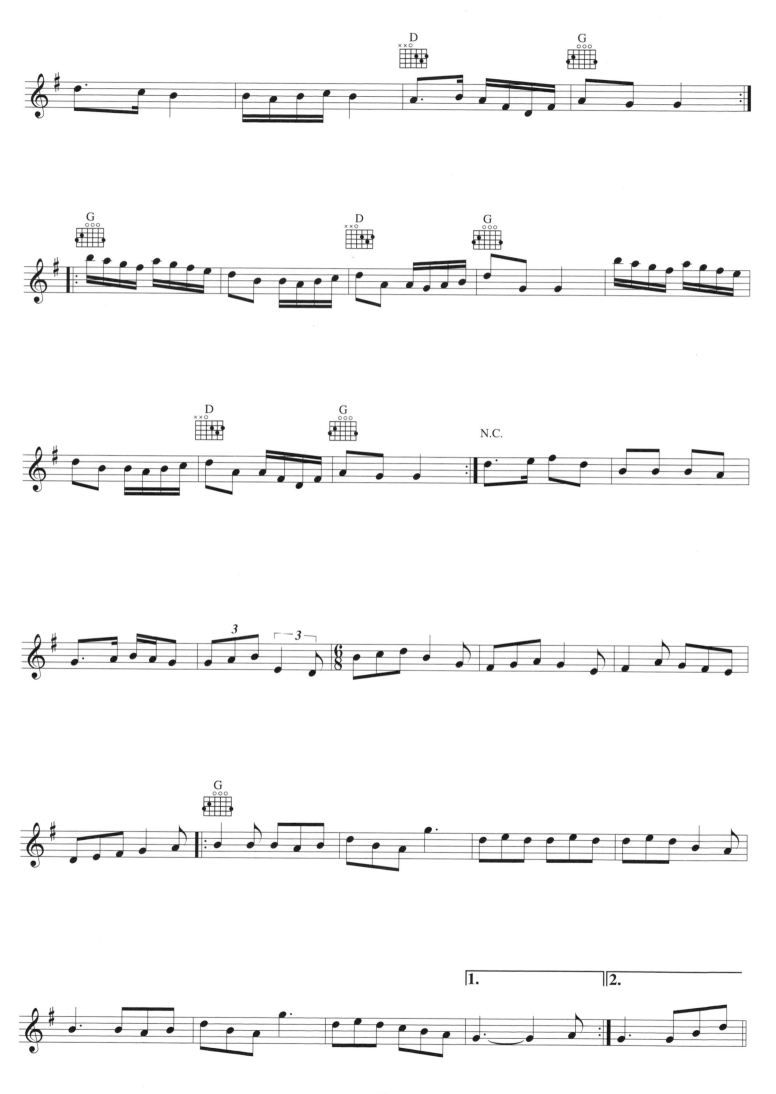

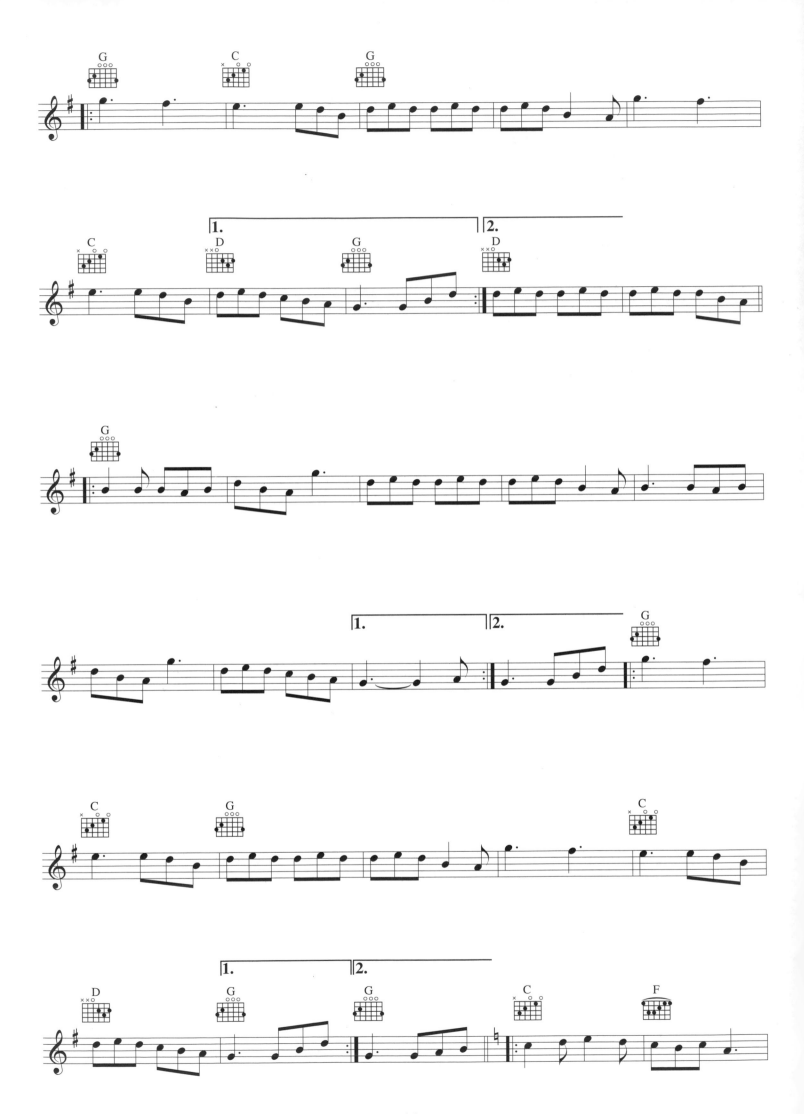

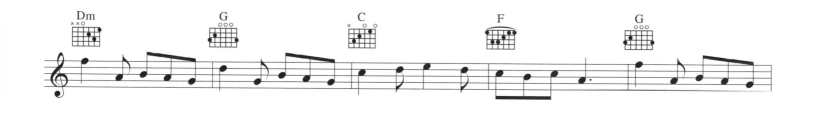

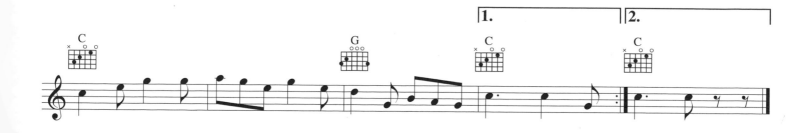

Chase Around The Windmill (Medley)

By P. Moloney, K. Conneff & M. Fay.

Toss The Feathers

By Paddy Moloney.

Segue

Ballinasloe Fair

By Paddy Moloney.

Cailleach An Airgid

By K. Conneff.

Segue

Cuil Aodha Slide

By P. Moloney.

The Pretty Girl

By M. Fay.

4° To Coda ⊕   D.%. al Coda   ⊕ Coda
(with repeats)

(Medley)
a. The Wind That Shakes The Barley

Traditional. Arranged by M. Tubridy.

b. The Reel With The Beryle

Traditional. Arranged by M. Tubridy.

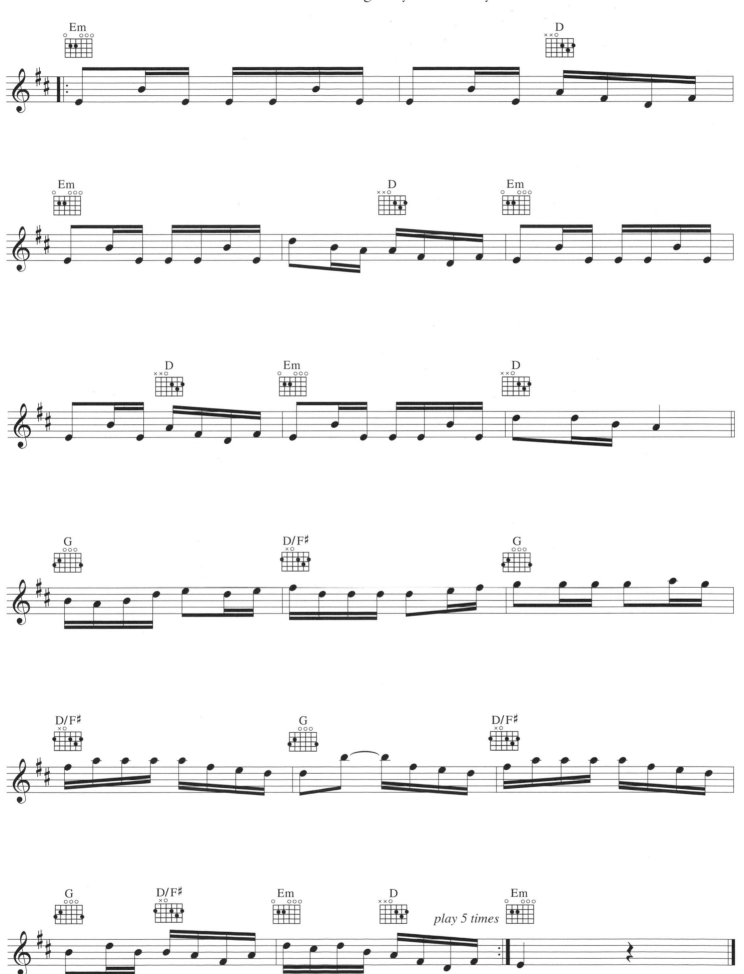